As if toward Beauty

for Alicia, Donald, and Elizabeth

As if toward Beauty

new poetry by
GWENDOLYN JENSEN

BIRCH
BROOK
PRESS

Softcover:
First edition
ISBN: 978-0-9915777-0-5
Library of Congress Catalog No: 2014940536

Hardcover:
limited to 100 copies

Art by Helen Febbo

The covers of both editions of this book
were printed letterpress at:

Birch Brook Press
PO Box 81
Delhi, NY 13753

To view our full catalog of books and art,
please pay a call on us at www.birchbrookpress.info
Email us at birchbrook@copper.net

CONTENTS

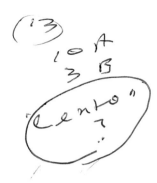

I AM LEARNING TO BE OLD

I am learning to be old.
It isn't hard, not as hard
as learning to be young, when
what lingers just before is hard
to grasp, alarmingly abundant.
I am learning to be old,
kept alive like Alexander
embalmed in honey to keep him fresh.
I am embalmed in the tangle
of my things, a dented car,   *CAR*
widescreen TV, and books enough.
And work, long, slow, humbling work,
the care that I must take, as if
the end can't be seen from here.
And friends (did I mention friends?),
dwindling, about to disappear.
I do not turn away.
I must watch them out of sight.
I am learning to be old.

FUGITIVE VISION

Let hurry tell
the story best
close the black door
push it tight
leave the listless
inside life
and out away
to otherwise
into halo's
hurried breath
stitch feathers on
a falcon's wing
venture haughty
to a planet
or moist star
let the mind
be uncollected
let courage seem
like carelessness
and so with voices
order is
a dumpish virtue
inhabit it
but have no dwelling there.

NIGHT RIDERS

In the wake of sleep they walk to where the mill run
runs through gnarly grasses, to where tomorrow's cows
will clamber down, making water dark and wide,
making muddy puddles, which like little fears,
draw upon a larger water. They cross to where
the horses stand, heads hung down, leaning in
upon themselves. What would it be to ride, to nuzzle
flat against a smooth warm neck? What would it be
to jump the fence, to go where air grows deep? Beyond them
lies a curve of farmhouse and its stubbled field,
and in the field a fox, high-tailed, alert, stands soft
among the brittle stalks, listening for a mouse,
aiming at a sound. And overhead there is
a filament of moon, the best of all the moons,
partial and complete, beyond the reach of ruin.

US HIGHWAY 50

And after that the road turns west
toward mountains, and toward clouds
that may be mountains, a saffron line,
penciled fluid, flat and straight.

Now comes the very sleep of travel
and the shimmering tribe of dreams,
fireflies dancing in a bottle,
murmuring to the sighing sun.

Buoyant linger time's illusion
and its cruel and useless beauty,
without hurry, without fear,
without the pain of destination.

SPARE PARTS

I modify sarcophagus
with paraphrase inseparable,
but with a sore esophagus–
diplodocus irreparable–

complements compound, appos-
itives resound, and only lonely gerunds
(while dining in Galapagos)
will find subjunctive pungency

in ways that will astound. Palaver's
susurration I mention sui generis–
you'll recognize the littermate of blather–
for when adjectives are generous,

adverbs make a crowd,
and that is all that grammar has allowed.

ROPES OF VEIN AND FRECKLED

Ropes of vein and freckled
Skin a comprehension
To feel the breathing nose
To nose with Abby dog
To know the warmth of tea
To touch the mind to think
More kindly of this flesh
And its lovely baseness.

SHALIMAR

She is damp from bathing, and her pores
Are open to the scent. It clings to her
As rain clings soft to earth. Her skin absorbs it,

Her sweat surrounds it with the urgency
Of arousal. Though she is faded, gaunt,
She still has thirst, and an urgency

That from nothing trembles. Her body's taut,
Her breasts are supple, with more of beauty than eye
Can bear. But she has netted slanting thoughts,

Like a boulder held from falling, sighing
For the stream below. And so she yields
To age, to its hushed steps and cruel disguises,

But not to weightlessness, not to the drowsy
Weightlessness of absence–the memory
Of time that needed no arousal.

DIE MALABARISCHEN WITWEN

Zum Flammentode gehn an Indusstranden
Mit dem Gemahl, in Jugendherrlichkeit,
Die Frauen, ohne Zagen, ohne Leid,
Geschmücket festlich, wie in Brautgewanden.

Die Sitte hat der Liebe Sinn verstanden,
Sie von der Trennung harter Schmach befreit,
Zu ihrem Priester selbst den Tod geweiht,
Unsterblichkeit gegeben ihren Banden.

Nicht Trennung ferner solchem Bunde droht,
Denn die vorhin entzweiten Liebesflammen
In Einer schlagen brünstig sie zusammen.

Zur süßen Liebesfeyer wird der Tod,
Vereinet die getrennten Elemente,
Zum Lebensgipfel wird des Daseins Ende.

Karoline von Günderrode (1780-1806)

THE WIDOWS OF MALABAR

A flaming death on Indus' banks they die,
Lying with their men, with youth and fire,
They do not suffer there, they have no fear,
In festive robes they come, as if new brides.

It understood the mind of love, this rite,
From shame and broken oaths, they were freed,
Death was consecrated to be their priest,
Death gave their bonds of love eternal life.

Their ties are not broken by a death,
What had been cut in two, love's flames
Put back together, the passion of one flame.

In this sweet festival of love, death
Unites broken elements, it unifies,
The end of life becomes the peak of life.

translated by G.J. and Monika Totten

TEE

You know how a shirt smells
a soft cotton shirt
gray short-sleeves
scooped neck
several days worn warm or cold
it doesn't matter

afterwards
you pull it off
sweat mainly dry
the shirt smells sweet
of grass
and moist and sun

and me, it smells of me
as when Abby dog
has her bath
and the kennel ties a kerchief on
as reward
or decoration

and after a week or so
we cut the kerchief off
put it in the wastebasket
but she takes it out
she keeps it close
a little longer

it's like that, isn't it?
this proof of life
not tossed away
the way kids
shake sand
from sandals

but cherished.

When I wake

When I wake, let me wake
to that rainy sometime day
we four girls spent together,
rolling up the rug and laughing,
the *Blue Danube* playing, bending
us to waltz, how very clumsy

we were then. Remember how,
every morning, early waking,
I'd stand mirror naked, bending
side to side to see my sometime
breasts, my not quite yets, my laughing
little birds. I had spent

so much time there waiting, spent
time dawdling, shirt pulled up. And how
I heard my nipples laughing
from the softness of their waking,
my unopened spices somewhere
on a shelf. And I saw bending

color under whiteness bending
blue, veins of blue all spent
with pink. I smelled good, somehow
older, all that lotion, how
I smoothed it on each waking.
On that dancing day of laughter,

tangled, curling, rolling laughter,
whirling all a-tangle, bending
toward each other, legs awake,
opening, closing, we were spending
all the whimsy of the world,
that's how we were that summer day.

Then I felt the pressure, something
pushing, my breasts were pushing. I laughed
at those brazen breasts and how
my green and narrow shirt was bent.
This is how I spent the day,
that rainy sometime day.

When I wake, let me wake to laughter,
let me bend and spend myself somehow,
for Venus is real, and the earth does move.

CONTINUING CARE

Our house is gone, my love, the things
that we assembled bit by bit,
scaffolding of memory
and loss. Old age is better here,
no need to buy a dozen eggs,
no need to buy an egg at all.   *age*
Just the eating we must do.

But the silence we call death
is loud without the work of living.
We run toward death. We run from death.
We run with death. We practice death.
The practices of death give daily
instances of its advantage.
Over us it will come.

LIEBE

O reiche Armuth! Gebend, seliges Empfangen!
In Zagheit Muth! in Freiheit doch gefangen.
    In Stummheit Sprache,
    Schüchtern bei Tage,
    Siegend mit zaghaftem Bangen.

Lebendiger Tod, im Einen sel'ges Leben
Schwelgent in Noth, im Widerstand ergeben,
    Genießend schmachten,
    Nie satt betrachten
Leben im Traum und doppelt Leben.

Karoline von Günderrode (1780-1806)

LOVE

O rich poverty! Giving, blissful taking!
In timidity, bold! In freedom, fettered.
      In speech, silence,
      In daylight, shy,
      In triumph, timid aching.

Living death, in one blissful life,
In starving, feasting; in yielding, denying,
      Enjoying yearning
      Famished observing,
Living in dream and doubled life.

translated by G.J. and Monika Totten

TWIN

Many start life doubled, more than one
might think. In the womb they have the ease
of close confinement and early reach to touch,
gesture's words brush up against the other.
If one of them is lost, the poverty
of one begins, the tyranny of one,
the frail tenacity of self enclosure–
as when a hungry man guards his dinner,
head down, arms stretched out around the plate.
But memory remains–a shudder of
familiarity, a text once learned
but lost through lack of recitation,
a wisp of cloud torn off by wind,
an unborn sorrow aborted early on.

I SING OF A BUS

I sing of a bus, the number 1 bus,
    from Dudley to Harvard Square,
the Harrison Avenue, Roxbury bus,
    we are all of us homeless there.

We fold to a pace set by another,
    we hold to our place to our fear,
we've learned whom to help, learned whom to shun,
    we're all of us homeless here.

I sing of a bus, the number 1 bus,
    it kneels to let some of us on,
the Harrison Avenue, Roxbury bus,
    it kneels to let some of us go.

I sing of a bus, the number 1 bus,
    from Dudley to Harvard Square,
the Harvard Square, MIT, Smoot Bridge bus,
    we are all of us homeless there.

Like horses and mules we've learned how to amble,
    professors and tourists and kids,
we take to the place the times that are ample,
    we're all of us homeless here.

I sing of a bus, the number 1 bus,
    it kneels to let some of us on,
the Harvard Square, MIT, Smoot Bridge bus,
    it kneels to let some of us go.

TO THE HOUSE SPARROWS, DISPOSSESSED

1.
Light was the weight you put on the ivy
your singing was light as your wings,
quiet the light the evening's blue light,
and no bird sings.

2.
Light was the weight you put on the ivy
when you clattering reared
back with your wings, you stalled, you sank,
you disappeared

3.
into the ivy you disappeared
small hours you slept away,
light was the weight you put on the ivy,
safe until day.

4.
Quiet this light this evening's blue light
 as you rear and fly headlong,
 spread back your wings, but shrieking you turn,
 for the ivy is gone.

5.
Light was the weight you put on the ivy
quiet the light as quiet as wings,
quiet the light the evening's blue light–
and no bird sings.

ABOUT THE WHITENESS
OF THE WHALE

A lamb, a combed white bear, an albatross,
driven snow, warm milk, an old man's sweat,
a string of pearls, a kitten's purr, the gloss
on drifted wood, cream cheese on a baguette,

white marriages, white wedding dresses, mourning
clothes, papal robes, the Ku Klux Klan,
white collar workers, summer's morning,
white noise, whitewash, white paper, white man,

lacquered demons known from birth,
pallid spirits of the gone, white
discarded skin of snakes, paper white
and weightless, open eyed and flung to earth.

SHALL I TEACH YOU
HOW TO HUNGER?

Shall I teach you how to hunger
How to howl at hunger's stare
The stare of hunger in the face
Deep within the breathing plane

Can I teach you how to hunger
Can I teach you you who've never
You who've never known a hunger
Your starched poverty of never

Hunger is a mouth half empty
Starveling withered undigested
Swallowing a weary never

Hunger is a snake half swallowed
Waiting weary undigested
Dangling from a withered mouth

snake

OFFICE

Resting, she leans back, coffee in her hands, changing and
unchanging screens before her, a mountain, a meadow full of
flowers, a laughing baby boy. She remembers how it used to be,
twists of carbon paper, filing, the sense of space between. How she
loved her I.B.M., how she learned to handle it, not to slap it into
gear, but be content to go along. Her computer is a more attentive
friend, so sturdy that the rain that scrapes the trash along the street
could never budge it. In the screen's inclination lie both yes and
no, no middle place. She does numbers. She feeds a thirst, a
dependency on numbers. She counts them, enters in their whirl
and heft, their tangle in the skein. She jolts them, and with a
hastening, all is brought to balance. Then she sends them out,
ironed flat and smooth as the brown muscle of a hill. Her kingdom
lies before her, paved, partitioned. It brings her joy, not the joy her
grandson felt with the first shadow of his puberty, but a practiced,
furnished joy, a joy she knows not how to name.

TALES FROM THE VIENNA WOODS

There is a mountain there, not much of one,   history?
But with the properties of all mountains,
Height beyond the usual knowing, and breadth
Beyond one's grasp, like a window facing east
That lets in all of morning.

They come, the rich, they come with those who serve them.
They come by horse and buggy, flowers in their hats,   —
And dogs that race beside. They come to hunt
The deer and shuddering boar, which though unmade,
Will be made again.

In the mountain, men dig a tunnel, steep
And down to where it's neither hot nor cold.
They come to take the gypsum there, and horses
Turn the winch and live in darkness, absorbed
They are by their surroundings.

The horses fear the dark and are blinded,
And the dark becomes their light. But those
Who gouge their eyes can smell the fear, they know
That even if a fear's unmade
It will be made again.

In war the mine becomes a factory.
They come to win that war, the rich, and those
Who serve them. They make one-person jets of wood,
Throwaway planes, with their throwaway pilots,
And their throwaway workers,

Marched to this new camp, weak ones strangled,
Others killed by gasoline injection.
Half-starved survivors forced to lend their backs,
Their limbs, their minds, their selves which if unmade,
Cannot be made again.

Now the mine's a lake. Tourists descend
To boats, to stables, to photographs of jets
And engineers. They come to play, the rich,
And those who serve them. They were unmade by war.
Now they're made again.

LIFE LESSON

It might have been a little gray dog,
curled tight under a shrub at the mall,
still loving the one who left it. It might
have been Dante inviting you to come
along with him. Or it might
have been a sudden waking, alone
in a room full of moonlight.

Or some other time, when you saw
the line between a skin of wind–
a wrongful thing so lightly winged
you could speak low of it, as in
putting a dog to sleep–and
that harder place, where things stick fast,
you can no longer shore against them.

CIRCUS

The elephants enter soft the way
the evening sky is sometimes soft
before a storm, when gravity
will hold its breath for thunderbeasts
whose curl and coil cannot be tamed.

Clowns rule circumference and pluck
disorder from the cloudy edge
of smile, strutting along a boundary
where luck, and luck's companion–sorrow–
stroll together arm in arm.

Beneath a firmament of tent
a child will swing again the simple
wooden swing in her backyard,
and gravity will hold its breath,
will hold her vast unquiet in its hands.

DOWSING

Soft and slow, the water moves,
Comely, cool, it lingers,
Fed by rain and snow it moves,
Unseen but shown in seeps and springs.

The rod is trembling, roughly forked,
Its edges roughly chanced
To find a curve–the way a lark
Finds curve in the air's resistance.

The rod's geometry will seek
The intimacy of strangers,
Stretching out and down to reach
Toward the harbor of black earth.

MAKER'S MARK:
AN ODE TO WHISKEY

I am grateful for the gift
of thirst, for drink is laughter,
laughter drink, a sparrow
rolling in a dust bath
stretching up and out
with dusty wings.

And to have no drink's to live
without reflection, closed
against the gift of thirst,
for the body's an imperfect
vessel for the spirit,
content to serve

God in safe places, not strong
enough to hold a goddess
tight enough to learn
her truths. And there are things
so delicate I dare not
pick them up,

like jellyfish scooped up
upon a sunny dock,
clear as light, without
reflection, as soon gone.
Even when the rain
darkens down

the sky, even when
the love makes me fear
the death, the path to joy
is never closed. Like
the path our mothers took,
it is not closed to us.

POWER

I serve porous circumstance,
and to this work I bring a boundless,
blazing self, but like a pond
whose silted grass and bottom mud
cannot be seen, my surface is smooth
and clear. If you look at me
you will see yourself.

I am mitered now, caparisoned,
like the elephant who bears
the true tooth of the true Buddha
ceremony becomes me.
I am the shape the trellis chooses,
trained tall, patterned predictable,
like the deepest blue clematis.

How will it be to leave? Will I
be eased by being nothing?
Someone else will drive my car
(once I killed a pigeon with that car).
The work will still be done.
It is assignable.
What portion of me is assignable?

-38-

HUCKLEBERRY FINN, CHAPTER 15

The river took the raft. It caught me,
Huck, in its breathing, breath
as thick as white as bodied demons
restless from the bottom rush,
surfacing and oozing out,
a tangle of horizons. I heard
you whoop, listened for the whoop's
return, but you, my Huck, were gone.

The fog-blind raft spiraled on,
I felt it scrape on island banks,
felt the overhanging branches
reach to sweep me off to drowning.
My soul stretched tight, I grabbed the oar.
It was damp and slightly singed
from where we keep it near the fire,
and scratched from times of hurry.

But it served me very well,
and I pushed away with it
against the banks and tangled roots.
Like an oarsman in a squall
who lets the useless tiller go,
I found my strength in push, not steer,
and the raft came free. But our oar
had shattered in my hands.

And then the fog was gone. I came
to open river, monstrous wide
the river was, along the shore

were vines as big, as old as trees,
climbing, stretching, up the trees,
a canopy that held the whole,
around the place that was river.
And overhead were stars.

I had forgotten stars. My child,
my child Elizabeth, how
she loved the stars. When I was home
sometimes, and after supper, she
would take my hand, and try to pull
me up and out, and say, or try
to say *Papa, come! Papa,*
see them! see them! see the stars!

Huck, could you see the stars?
Or had the river drawn you down
to drowning, down to sludge and muck
where catfish large as dogs lie waiting?
And so I floated, curled into
a knot of seeking. I slept while giants
angry in their sleep, muttered
in the night like silent thunder.

And when I woke, here you were,
my honey chile, not lost, not drowned,
the same old Huck. I wept and told you
what had happened. But you told me
it was a tangle-headed dream.
You asked me to interpret it,

and I made up a pretty tale,
made my terror safe and useful.

But when I'd finished, the stars had gone,
dawn had come, and on our raft
were torn-off branches, leaves, and vines,
and pieces of our shattered oar.
I had made a dream for you
from things that you will never see,
things you had not seen, things
that you pretended were not there.

You shamed your Jim.
You fooled my tangled head.
I had shown you fear
that took the measure of my love.
And you laughed at me.
You made my love unneedful,
awkward, an excess.
You turned it into dirt.

Now you stand before me,
you ask me to forgive you.
My child, my child,
you're just a boy.
To say sorry,
that is what a man might do.
Take my hand.
I want no shame on you or me.

AFTER YOU DIED

But of course I didn't know you had died, not right away. I was at a meeting, drove home, and Father told me, and we embraced for you, and for each other. We had to go to you, we had to arrange for what was left. The woman who cleaned for us arrived, and I was abrupt with her when she asked a question about her day's work. Our daughter died, I said, and we must go now. We flew to you, to your house. We had spoken the night before. The pain had moved into your brain you said, it hurt so much. Did you plan your death? Or did you let death come to you? And where were you? What happens when a person dies? You were at the morgue. And did we want to see you? No, we did not. I hope you do not mind. It was just an automatic response, a reflex really, but you must have been cold by then, and even sick you were so very warm. And then we went to bed, the bed where you had died the night before. A friend had washed the sheets and made it up again. When you bought this little house you told us you were startled on your first night to see the bedroom ceiling full of stars, a luminescence that held the light of day. And so we slept, full of thought, and overhead a field of stars.

HARVARD SQUARE

Deep below us, far from morning, where
The train has not yet come, where commuters
Listless breathe the musty tunnel air,
The supple track is humming, keening, brooding
Surface restlessness. Then the bruising
Train, all wind and piss, grinds through the camber
Of the curve. Brakes groan and bite and smooth,
And the train spreads itself to stand,
Like a river rising, flat upon the land.

train
bus
can

THE GIFT

To the wearer
scent smells only
when first sprayed,
a cloud walked through
and then gone.
But for another
briefly met
the scent is his
to spin into
a ludic wild
a ludicrous
and random joy.

So it is
a mockingbird
gravely pregnant
with a song
takes the songs
of other birds
to spin its song
a mating call
or a whispered
nesting song
capacity
enlarged.

RETIREMENT

He had woven out a net, had woven
    with the measure of his touch and tongue,
    loose, exuberant, he had thrown it
    out upon the width of day, had flung it
    forth, had given to his time a tongue,
    had worked had lived largely on this earth;
    his emblems now are gone, his songs are sung,
    the children of his listening. He is
    a songbird caught in a net, its head hung down,
a stranger murmuring to himself, turbulent, unheard.

A CAR HAS SUMMER IN IT

A car has summer in it, and a boy
can flit full-footed, nimble through the streets,
a sheen of sound unfurled behind, sleek
and bristling as a howling cat, passing
car to car, open, wide, and shared.

A car has summer in it, and the smells
a summer carries, the hot sweat of pizza,
the gritty sweat of warm beer and sun,
and morning smells, the *Globe* or *Herald*, pitched
just right, to a dancer's soundless landing.

A car has summer in it, and the years
worn young. It has the poise a good machine
can carry, the buoyancy of line and shape.
It holds a record of the unrecorded.
It is the marker, a marker he can touch.

MONEY

Money is a story told at suppertime, how Great-Grandfather
bought his shop, married, mastered deprivation. Money is our way
to talk, our way to sing. Money is a bucket dancing in the wind.
Money is our duty and our righteousness, the direction of our lives
together, what holidays or whether, what charities or whether.
And the children have small say in this, like our dog, who chases
cars, but cannot drive. And when we hide ourselves from each
other (as we do, always sometimes, rarely never) money tells us
what we know about each other. Money is the family's beauty,
bristling with delight, the wonder of a way of walking where there
is no path, a growing place, the tip of a fingernail, the froth at the
edge of the universe.

THE TIE

The razor pulls his unborn face,
the mirror mirrors warmth of waking,
breath of last night's beer. Today
he'll wear the lilac tie, lilac
as a pigeon's strut when almost
all the crumbs are gone. It is
without the softening of line
or regimental stripe, a smooth
and certain surface, of the sort
his father ties, high-handed, sure.

What he is is as may be,
what he will be will pick its way,
the way a hawk first takes its hood,
eyelids sewn, yielding wildness,
learning how to take its meat
from the trainer's hand, and how
to soar to purpose not its own.
He soothes his damp and private parts,
tucks them safe away. He buttons
his shirt, lifts his chin, and ties the tie.

THE WEDDING PICTURE

I can see you in the picture, Mommy.
By the night-light I can see you swirled
and garlanded, coming down the aisle

My dress is white and garlanded, and I
am coming down the aisle. I am coming
down to get you, my darling baby girl.

Why did you leave so soon?   I must have hurt you
being born, hurt you coming out.
I am sorry if I made you cry.

I will kiss your tummy, that lovely slippery
tummy. I'll make you laugh, touch you warm
between your legs, between your every toe.

I would have climbed down to you, but
your coffin had been closed, and there were shapes
in that darkness, and pale sound.

Daughter! Daughter! Help me down!
I will keep you safe from darkness
and pale sound.

Why did you go?
Where did you go? Why did you leave me?
What is death that you died?

Daughter! Daughter! Take my hand!
I will sit there on your bed,
I'll brush your dark and tangled hair.

I'm sleepy now.
I'll make space soon.
My dolls won't mind.

PARALLEL PARKING

mighty Contests rise from trivial Things
                                    -- Alexander Pope

Fear of ticket, fear of tow,
anger if a space too small,
I find a spot and back it in
–sure instinct of the half-shut eye–
bump against the car in front,
then bump the one behind, each thwack's
the measure of capacity,
which like the depth of joy or sorrow
is not proportioned to the cause;
but in this place where boundary matters,
in this poor infected world,
I can die in Metaphor,
or I can die in Song.

CARS
↓
bumpers of
life

SUPPOSE A POEM

Suppose a poem,
by itself,
abandoned,
the poet gone,
to another
poem perhaps,
or to a woman
not his wife.

Suppose a poem
is restless, open
to the whisper
of dry wheat,
and delicate
as ocean sun
that dwells on nothing
but horizon.

Suppose a poem
be in repose,
all its parts
are stitched and hemmed,
a simple soldier
borne along
by wounds that heal
but never close.

DIRECT REPORT

His days are interchangeable,
like flakes of snow, or commuters
on a silent bus, resembling
nothing but themselves—
when to do, when to wait,
when to leave undone,
which word will say the no the best.
The texture of his work is subtle,
the way a sailor finds
the necessary slope,
not head on, but swimming
with the forward breeze.

When a different person comes
to work behind his desk,
she will find traces there
of his way of doing,
something of him will remain,
the way a simple courtesy
remains, long after reason's gone.
Like a farmer who unearths
an arrowhead, she will wonder
at its maker, and at the bones,
the murmurous bones,
that lie beneath her feet.

VORZEIT, UND NEUE ZEIT

Ein schmahler rauher Pfad schien sonst die Erde.
Und auf den Bergen glänzt der Himmel über ihr,
Ein Abgrund ihr zur Seite war die Hölle,
Und Pfade führten in den Himmel, und zur Hölle.

Doch alles ist ganz anders nun geworden,
Der Himmel ist gestürzt, der Abgrund ausgefüllt,
Und mit Vernunft bedekt, und sehr bequem zum gehen.
Des Glaubens Höhen sind nun demolieret.
Und auf der flachen Erde schreitet der Verstand,
Und misset alles aus, nach Klafter und nach Schuen.

Karoline von Günderrode (1780-1806)

THEN, AND NOW

Once earth seemed a rough, tight path.
And in the mountains Heaven glowed,
And at earth's side, a deep abyss was Hell,
And paths led up to Heaven, and to Hell.

But now everything's entirely altered,
Heaven has collapsed, the abyss filled in
And paved with reason, and very easy walking.
The heights of faith have been demolished.
And knowledge strides across the smooth flat earth,
And measures everything, in fathoms, cords, and feet.

translated by G.J. and Monika Totten

IT IS COLD TONIGHT

Air lies soft, soft and careful, taking
old man's steps, light upon the earth,
suspended, as if turned and turning in
upon itself. Air lies quiet, taking
time, as if at a bus stop, patient,
not caring who the others are, but certain
that the bus will come. Air lies curled
in the graceful shape indifference takes–

as if it would not need the trees awaiting
early snow; as if it would not hear
the murmuring houses, lit inside, would
not see the cars, drifting toward a place.
As if its place is not here,
but there, where cold is understood.

WHOM DO I TELL WHAT HAPPENED ON THE EARTH?

(a cento*)

Whom do I tell what happened on the earth?
The sea is everywhere without a shore
as though by a giant wave lifted up,
and dolphins take possession of the woods.
Many ingenious lovely things are gone
whose beauty's silent power stopped my heart–
hammered gold and gold enameling
glistening in the marble palace steps.

I sleep on the top of a high and giddy mast,
I wear man's smudge and share man's smell,
I make no rhyme in praise of nothingness.
I've all a man can carry into death,
the grass below–above, the vaulted sky,
and when I wake I cry to dream again.

* line sources, in this order: Milosz, Ovid, Ashbery, Ovid, Yeats, Logue, Yeats, Pound, Bishop, Shakespeare, Hopkins, Milosz, Flannery O'Connor, Clare, Shakespeare

TRESPASS

How clean you smell,
your skin is smooth,
your hairy thicket,
once so dense and thorned,
is more cobweb now,
though not without intent;
and the spider waits,
the web will do its work.

It must be trespass what I do,
not the trespass of a hunter
or a fisher, not the trespasses
we say in church,
but trespass of the eye and hand,
which move across the surface of a life,
the felt surface of a life
that is not mine.

About the Authors/Artist

Gwendolyn Jensen was born in 1936 and grew up in Lansdowne, PA. She began writing poems when she retired in 2001 from Wilson College (Chambersburg, Pennsylvania) where she had served as president for ten years. Her Bachelors degree is from the University of Hartford, her Masters from Trinity College (Hartford), and her Ph.D. from the University of Connecticut.

After teaching history at the University of New Haven she moved into administrative work serving as graduate dean at the University of New Haven, and then as academic dean, first at Western State College (Gunnison, Colorado) and then at Marietta College (Marietta, Ohio).

Birthright, her first book of poems, was published in 2011 by Birch Brook Press as a letterpress edition and had a second printing in 2012.

She and her late husband Gordon Jensen have three children, and two grandsons. She lives in Cambridge, Massachusetts.

*

Helen Febbo's work has been shown in the Arden Gallery (Boston) and the Katherine Rich Perlow Gallery (New York City) and is in the permanent collection of the Berkshire Museum (Pittsfield, Massachusetts).

*

Karoline von Günderrode (1780-1806) was a German romantic poet who wrote strong lyrical poems of love and death. She published a great deal of her work, despite her early death, a suicide.

*

Monika Totten is a retired scholar of German literature with a Harvard Ph.D. in German literature and language. She has published and presented papers on Günderrode.

About the Book

As if toward Beauty was published as a "hybrid edition" featuring a cover printed letterpress on a hand-fed Chandler & Price press at Birch Brook Press from handset metal type and an engraving made from Helen Febbo's original artwork. Interior text was typeset on a computer and printed offset in 12 pt. Palatino Linotype, a font designed by Hermann Zapf, and named after the Italian master of calligraphy, Giambattista Palatino.

Acknowledgments

I wish to thank Helen Febbo, Cola Franzen, Gordon Jensen, Emily Romney, Carol Steinhagen, Monika Totten, members of the Woodberry Translation Group, the editors of Birch Brook Press, and the editors of the following journals, where some of these poems first appeared:

"About the Whiteness of the Whale," and "After You Died," *Amarillo Bay;* "Money," *Amethyst Arsenic;* "Tee," *The Evansville Review;* "Night Riders," *Freshwater;* "To the House Sparrows, Dispossessed," *Harvard Divinity Bulletin;* "Harvard Square," *The Licking River Review;* "The Tie," *The Hollins Critic;* "The Widows of Malabar," and "Whom Do I Tell What Happened on the Earth?" *Measure;* "Dowsing," *Nashville Review;* "Parallel Parking," *OVS Magazine;* "It is Cold Tonight," and "When I Wake," *Red Ochre Press;* "I Am Learning to Be Old," *Salamander;* "Shalimar," *Sanskrit: Literary Arts Magazine;* "Love," *Tears in the Fence;* "US Highway 50," and "The Wedding Picture," *The Foliate Oak Literary Magazine;* "Spare Parts," *The Harvard Review;* "I Sing of a Bus," *Rio Grande Review;* "Circus," *Valparaiso Poetry Review;* "Retirement," *Wild Violet Magazine;* "Suppose a Poem," *Word Riot.*